HABITS FOR SUCCESS IN BUSINESS

The roadmap to higher business performance

ROXANNE MARTIN

Table of content

ROXANNE MARTIN

INTRODUCTION

There is no substitute for time, education and being in action to take a business to the next level. Through time, and increasing your expertise, it is possible to add value to people's lives. Sooner, if not later, you will become the expert. You cannot do something for years and years and not expect to become great at it. The key is to find something you love doing and keep at it.

Keeping at a business, even if you love it, usually requires stamina, patience and perseverance. It is the ability to allow growth in the form of change. Over time you will see what works and what does not work. You will get feedback from other people who will help you evaluate your business. Feedback from other people is very valuable information. Learn from it.

To take your business to the next level keep refining what you are doing. Keep measuring your success and tweaking it for the better. Give up some ideas or parts of your business completely if you have to, but keep building and reshaping the rest. Go with the times and the flow of the economy and what successes your business already has, and keep striving for excellence. In other words, find out what people are buying and the price ranges that are affordable for them and sell that.

If you are just starting out, and some people would say that starting out a business is from years one to four, you will have to have a plan for building your success. Sometimes building your business can be in the form of getting educated, as many people aquire university degrees for their careers. Whatever you are doing, whether that be getting educated and/or creating your business, there has to be a plan and a time frame to aquire money.

Do not keep putting money into ideas that are not generating cash for you. Stop the outflow and take a hard look at your business plan. Work at the part of your plan that brings in money. Some people may have to go back to basics at this point or even come up with another business plan. Some people find out they have too many business ideas floating around, too many stakes in the fire so to speak, so they need to concentrate and to focus on only one or two--the most lucrative ones. If more education is needed, focus on completing this. Once, one or two aspects of your business are flourishing, you can always add from there.

Taking your business to the next level requires personal growth. Why? "If you always do what you have always done you cannot expect different results."(This is the definition of insanity.) To get to the next level you have to do something different. The ability to do something different is personal growth

If, for example, what you find to do different adds exponential growth and sales to your business, you would have most likely done this a long time ago. Therefore, keep refining your own knowledge and expectation of what actions you can take to allow progress so that your business grows. Keep in mind that sometimes your business will grow slowly and sometimes your business will take off like wild fire and grow rapidly. When this happens, it is wonderful; you will know that all of your hard work is paying off.

HABITS FOR PERSONAL SUCCESS

What is your record for meeting goals that you set? Do you often fall short of the goal? Do you start out excited but lose interest quickly?

The following are simple daily habits that will help you succeed

Find Your Passion

Too often we take on goals because someone else thinks we should be a certain way.

Maybe your husband thinks you should be skinnier or your coworker talked you into signing up for a triathlon. Your boss might have coerced you into agreeing to aim for a certain level of sales or productivity, or perhaps you feel pressured by society in general to set a specific goal.

The key to success is to tap into your genuine, internal passion. That means you need to identify goals that truly inspire and excite you, goals that come from within.

If someone else has set a goal for you and you don't have the authentic desire to achieve it (let's say your parents say you must get A's in college, or they won't pay your way), you need to get in touch with something authentic that will motivate you. Perhaps your fear of living in poverty could inspire you, or your desire to graduate without student loan debt.

Habit one to success is to daily remind yourself of that genuine passion that will fuel your fire.

Aim High

Do you want to lose ten pounds? Then set your goal for fifteen.

Do you want to make $100,000 a year? Set your goal for $110,000.

Most of us have trouble seeing a goal through from start to finish. That's why it's wise to shoot for something higher than you need to achieve. Then, if you lose steam three-quarters of the way to the goal, you will still have achieved enough to be satisfied.

Get Specific with Goal-Setting

People who are in the habit of setting vague goals (like "I want to lose weight") are far less likely to succeed in meeting those goals than people who set specific goals (like "I want to lose twenty pounds.")

Become a person who refuses to accept a vague goal as a real goal. Instead, force yourself to think through the details and to get specific. Write down those specific goals and keep them somewhere you can see them every day.

Set Small, Attainable Goals

After you've gotten specific about your overarching goal, you'll want to break it down into small, achievable goals that will lead up to completing the end goal.

These goals should be practical things that can be done every single day and can, in and of themselves, become habits.

For example, let's say you want to lose twenty pounds. You will then need to research weight loss and come up with a weekly goal, let's say one pound per week. You will then need to schedule out what you will do each day to achieve this goal.

Will you log your calorie consumption on an online calorie counter? Will you check in with a weight loss buddy every day about menu choices? Will you perform some exercise each day? If so, what kind of exercise will you perform each day that week?

Plan out small, reasonable actions you can take. Then check them off as you finish them. Prepare for off days, when you won't be able to meet your goal for the day, and accommodate for that by planning more effort on other days.

If you get in the habit of taking a specific action, you will be far more likely to achieve your goals.

Address Your Weaknesses

Most of us have at least one weakness that we'd really like to change. Perhaps you are afraid of public speaking or can't figure out how to dress professionally, and as a result, you are insecure in a professional environment.

Instead of avoiding public speaking or settling for an unprofessional job, challenge yourself to tackle your weakness head-on.

Hire a stylist to help you learn how to shop, dress and style your hair professionally. Invest upfront in overcoming weaknesses that undermine your self-confidence, and you will set yourself for a more successful life overall.

Laugh at Your Mistakes

What is your first reaction when you've realized you've made a minor mistake?

If it's to laugh at yourself, you're on the right track. If you take yourself too seriously, you will be more likely to get discouraged and give up. It's important to let mistakes and failures roll off your back so you can get back on the proverbial horse again.

Make it a habit of laughing – even if it's forced laughter – at yourself when you blow it. By refusing to get down, you'll find the strength to persevere until you've met your goal.

Enjoy the Journey

Some have been tempted to think they will be so much happier once they've met a goal, only to discover later that really, their life is only marginally improved. Wait a couple of months after achieving the goal, and in most cases, you won't feel all that much happier than you were before you tackled the goal.

That's because we adjust emotionally to whatever our current conditions are. The real satisfaction occurs while we are mid-pursuit of a goal or dream.

Why?

The challenge and all those mini-successes along the way are more exciting than the result when we finally "arrive." While pursuing a new goal, we usually learn a lot, meet new people, figure out that we are capable of more than we previously knew and experienced a lot of drama, both good and bad.

Become a person who daily reminds yourself to enjoy the journey. You'll be happier and more likely to see the journey to the actual destination.

Find Accountability Partners

Accountability is one of the most powerful tools for meeting goals. When someone else knows what your goals are and is willing to hold you accountable, you will find the strength to follow through in situations when you might have compromised or made excuses.

That's why you will benefit if you formally commit to a support/accountability system. You might want to join an online forum, start attending a support group like Alcoholics Anonymous, hire a life coach or agree with a friend who is just as committed to your success as you are.

Once you get your support system set up, establish a habit of checking in with your accountability system daily. That may mean posting a quick report online as to whether or not you took a scheduled step towards your goal or talking to your support friend.

Daily accountability will help you succeed.

Track Your Progress
If you want to succeed, you'll need to keep track of your daily progress in a concrete fashion. Set tangible goals such as:

- I will write 500 words every day (If you want to write a book)
- I will exercise five days a week (if you want to get in shape)
- I will devote the first thirty minutes of my day to building my online business
- I will pack my lunch of healthy foods every day (if you want to improve your health)

Make a chart or spreadsheet of these mini goals and then mark off how well you fulfill your commitments each day. If you get in the habit of tracking your progress, you will find success is that much easier to achieve.

Make Your Goals Public Knowledge
We're naturally predisposed to want to look good. That's why going public with goals (and success or failure to take steps to meet goals) works so well.
Go public with your goal, stating your plan on a public forum such as your workplace, a group of friends, an online forum or a support group.

Some people find posting on a blog helps them since the audience of the entire internet can be quite convincing. After all, you don't want to fail publically, right?

Make it a habit of posting details of your progress in one public arena, even if it's on a forum under a screen name. You'll be amazed at how much you'll want to have good news to post each day, even if the people witnessing your journey don't know your real name.

Follow an Established Path

Once you've determined what your goal is, you need to find someone or something to follow. That someone could be an expert in the field, an excellent training book, a training class or an idol who will inspire you.

If you try to reinvent the wheel by yourself, you'll end up making mistakes or hitting roadblocks you could have avoided.

Find a book, online program or mentor and craft your plan to the success of that example. This will also help you believe it can be done – after all, you're just following in the footsteps of someone who has already succeeded!

Take Risks

If you want to grow, you have to take risks.

This is simply the nature of our being. When stretched, we find out we can do so much more than we imagined we could, but when we are not challenged, we don't usually push ourselves enough to find out what we could achieve.

You can apply this basic principle to your goal-seeking efforts. Make a habit of taking on the bigger of two challenges when presented options.

For example, let's say you want to train for a marathon. Your friend stops by for a run and gives you the option: Do you want to try to push for extra miles today, or do you want to go for an easy run. Unless you think you'll risk an injury, the wise answer is to go for the extra miles, especially since you might not push yourself as much later in the week when working out on your own.

Likewise, take on work challenges, creative challenges and interpersonal opportunities when they arise. This will get you in the habit of testing your limits.

Set High Stakes and Rewards

Are you at a point where you realize you're not motivated to succeed? Then you need an effective stick and carrot system in place.

You can set stakes high by:

- Accepting a bet (monetary investment)

- Going public with your commitment (blog, pool with coworkers, support group)
- Signing up for a commitment that will require you have achieved at least some success (signing up for a race)

Ask yourself what would matter to you, and then use that as motivation to force you to meet your goal.

Focus on One Area at a Time

One of the biggest mistakes people make is to take on more than one goal at a time.

We all want to believe we can improve everything in our lives at once, but you've got to realize this truth: you have these bad habits or have not achieved these goals for a reason. They are probably very hard for you to achieve or you'd have already accomplished them all! That's why you need to make it a habit never to take on more than you can tackle at once.

If you want to write a screenplay, then you probably will need to stop putting in extra hours at your job, cut down on socializing and invest emotional and mental energy in thinking about the play.

If you want to quit smoking, you probably shouldn't try to lose weight at the same time.

Commit to one goal for an extended period, and make sure all other goals are secondary or nonexistent for the time being. Give yourself self-grace in the other areas and focus all of your attention on improving in this one, specific area.

Don't Over-Commit

Have you ever noticed that other people often derail your good intentions to work on your goal?

For example, you might have planned to devote eight hours to your new affiliate marketing business this week. Perhaps you promised yourself you would write and post six new blog posts and outline that email campaign you planned on launching.

However, you were asked by your sister if you could watch her kids one night, and then your boss told you that you "really should attend" a happy hour or dinner with your coworkers who are in from out of town for the week. Your work out buddy begged you to please run a race with him on Saturday, and your daughter asked for a roller skating sleepover party.

Before you know it, all eight hours of your time have vanished into thin air.

How can you avoid this?

Develop the habit of asking for time to "think it over" before committing.

You can use the line, "Let me check my calendar and get back to you." Then make yourself wait at least 24 hours before responding to requests.

You may find that your sister finds someone else to watch her kids and a bunch of your coworkers decline the happy hour invitation, making it more acceptable for you to also say no. Your work out buddy may be fine doing the race with or without you, and your daughter might get invited to someone else's house – freeing you up even more.

Collect Inspiring "Totems"

Not sure what a totem is? A totem is a physical item that reminds you of something important. It could be something as small as a lucky coin or as big as a statue.

Have you ever noticed that some people collect things that inspire them? That's exactly what you'll want to do. Collect physical items that remind you of your goal and will inspire you to persevere.

For example, if your goal is to run a marathon, you might want to collect things like a shoe keychain, medals, and t-shirts from races you've run, inspirational posters, a pebble you retrieved from your shoe on a particularly good run, etc.

Keep these totems where you can see them often. They'll keep you focused on your goal.

TOP 5 WAYS TO STAY MOTIVATED TO BUILD YOUR HOME BASED BUSINESS

Consider yourself lucky if you are working from home and trying to run your own home based business. It has its perks and benefits, like no commute, no overhead expenses, the flexible hours, and the best of all, becoming your own boss. This means that you are accountable to no one but yourself, so no fear of getting written up, laid off or fired.

But along with these advantages comes the responsibility of building your own home based business. You have to deal with the good as well as the bad things that go with it. It is not all a bed of roses. One of the biggest challenges and obstacles that people in this kind of business run into is how to stay motivated. When you first started your business, you were overflowing with enthusiasm, energy and passion, and there was no stopping you. Then lately, you begin to wonder where that love went.

Everyone who has a home based business goes through a slump occasionally, and it is normal. The challenge is how to stay motivated and keep going to be able to succeed and reach your goals. Some people also stay content with just getting an income to get by, and don't aim to take their business to the next level.

Here are five ways to light the fire again, and hopefully, take you out of the rut that you are in.

Be organized and set a schedule

Nothing can drain one's energy and motivation more than a cluttered office and lack of schedule. There must be a semblance of a daily schedule to keep you going. If possible, create a "to do" list based on a daily, weekly and monthly schedule. The task could be as simple as organizing the papers in your desk, to difficult ones like writing a page content for your website. The goal is to give you a sense of accomplishment as you complete each task.

Set and reassess your goals

Setting goals is important if you are running a home based business to keep your mind and energy focused. They don't have to be large and grand ones, start with small and attainable ones. Take the time to reassess and monitor these goals regularly, and make the necessary adjustments.

Change it up a bit during slow business times

There will be times when your business might slow down but don't let this discourage you. Think of other ways to augment your income like doing some freelance job or short-term assignments or look for other business opportunities that you can integrate into your current business. Aside from the added income, it will also keep you occupied.

Get out of the house and network

One way to stay motivated is to network with others. Working from home can be lonely sometimes and facing your computer everyday can get boring. Surely, there are other people in your business community who can offer advice about your business. You could also gather some leads, and get to socialize and feed your soul. You need to breathe some fresh air sometimes even if it is running errands or meeting friends for lunch to keep you energized and inspired.

Celebrate your successes

Finally, be kind to yourself and write down a list of rewards that you will give yourself for accomplishing a certain goal or milestone. Post it somewhere where you will be reminded every day. You deserve more than a pat on the back for all the hard work you have put in your home based business.

Remember that you deserve success, so keep yourself motivated. You need to be constantly doing these steps to be on track and to reap the benefits of the sacrifices you are doing.

OTHER SMALL HABITS FOR SUCCESS IN BUSINESS

Make staying in shape non-negotiable.
Staying in shape is a habit, and takes priority on a daily basis. I don't allow the state of the business to get in the way of exercising. In fact, I schedule a time to exercise in my head at the beginning of the week and every day to ensure I know when I will be working out. When I travel, I pack my gym clothes first, thinking about the week ahead and planning the schedule of workouts. Just like putting money away for retirement when you are young and making it a habit, pay yourself first when it comes to exercise.

Do the most important thing first
In order to ensure you accomplish your priorities for the day, you must do the most important thing first, before you leave for the office. A lot of people call this 'eating the frog.' It's hard, but you have to do your best to do that every morning.

Talk to someone new about your product every day.

Don't just sit in your ivory tower--go out and learn what people are thinking about your product. Talk to people at grocery stores, at baseball games, and even your kids' games (which might annoy them).

Ask people what you can do for them.

To receive great support and help you must be an even greater supporter and helper. Starting a business is extremely challenging, and requires the daily help and guidance of investors, partners, and peers. Too often entrepreneurs fall into the trap of constantly asking things of others while offering little in return. It's bad form and an easy way to burn bridges. But if you can be a thought leader and resource for your peers, and if you go out of your way to help them, they will ultimately go out of their way to help you. There are few greater compliments than having someone say, 'I would do anything for that person.' This habit will make that person you.

Learn to delegate.

Delegating well is an art form, deceptively difficult, always improved, and usually learned the hard way. Pay too much attention and you micromanage; pay too little attention and it seems like you don't care. Start by delegating work where the key is to clearly verbalize your expectations, recognize the difference between something that's worse and something that's different from how you would have done it, and make sure to avoid hero mode where you shoulder the largest burden.

Get enough sleep.
Lack of sleep can contribute to increased stress and poor decision making. Have a sleep regiment that you stick to whenever possible. One hour before bedtime: No work, phones, or computer screens, because the blue light from screens has been shown to interfere with sleep cycles. A relaxing routine helps you sleep and be the most effective the next day.

Use tech to turn off.
Have recurring calendar invites--one mid-morning, one at lunch, and one mid-afternoon--that tell you: 'Take a beat.' It will remind you to slow down and stop what you're doing for about five minutes. This is when you could let your mind wander and absorb the events of that day or morning. You'll find it amazing how frequently those calendar invites pop up exactly when you need them most.

Walk and talk.

It's easy to hurry through your day, whether walking from meeting to meeting or answering copious emails and phone calls while chained to your desk. Try stopping to talk to every third person you come across daily as you are walking through the office. Why assign a number rather than just making a general effort to chat with everyone you pass? The rule ensures that you have a quality conversation and connect with a few different people throughout the day, rather than building a reputation for talking any person's ear off that crosses your path. Great conversations lead to stronger relationships and ideas.

Hire people with high emotional intelligence.

Being book smart is not enough as an employee of a very successful company. A great company needs people who work well with others. The world has become so dependent on working across functions and sharing information that any low-EQ/high-IQ hires need not apply.

Don't panic in the face of unexpected challenge.

When faced with an unforeseen challenge, which is inevitable, your first step should be to stay calm, search for solutions--not excuses--and to relentlessly pursue execution of that solution.

Check in with one employee at random.
Strike up an unexpected conversation with one different employee every day (if you have any). It shows that what they do matters, and it's fun to learn what they're working on, what they're excited about, and what questions they have about the company. There's no better way to keep a pulse on your company's progress."

Invest in mentors.
Whether through phone, email, or coffee meetings, spend a portion of your time each day connecting with people and absorbing outside insight. You can do this in two ways. The first is to offer your help to others. Working with people who are building businesses can drive your own creativity. The second is to receive help from others. Having a network of influencers with whom you can be extremely transparent, can shape some of the hardest decisions you'll have to make and might bring to light new ideas you might have otherwise overlooked. The return here far outweighs the time you will invest in these relationships every day.

Meet for lunch with five people from random departments across the company.

Why five people? Because that's how many can fit in a car. You can try to do something that's delicious and off the beaten path. When your company starts growing very fast, it's very important to make sure that you keep strong your culture of open, direct, and honest communication, as this could be one of the key reasons for your growth. Lunch Buddies also help people get to know others in the company whom they might not cross paths with.

Read things unrelated to your business.

Some days try historical or science fiction. Other times, try reading academic or medical papers or anything that you might enjoy and is different from your regular reads. No matter how far from the business these readings may take you, you will learn things and come up with "out of the box" ideas that inspire and inform your work.

Prepare mentally before going to work.

Spend time listening to motivational tapes that enable you to visualize what you want to have happen that day. Through this process, you will be able to rid yourself of the normal worries and stresses that come with running a business while being laser-focused on the positive outcome envisioned for that day. As a result, you will have experiences that some might call miraculous when applying this steadfast.

Intentionally daydream.
Every day, in my drive to and from work, I purposely shut off the radio, put my cell phone away, and allow myself to daydream. Many view daydreaming as a useless activity. For me, daydreaming allows me to re-energize my battery, which helps me focus when I need to and be present to those who need my attention. It also fuels creativity. Oftentimes, important ideas, connections, and realizations come during and after I intentionally daydream. You should try it sometimes.

Live in the question instead of the conclusion.
When you are walking down the halls of conclusion, it is hard to see the doors of opportunity and possibility. Many organizations focus on reporting what is not working versus what is possible. Already overextended leaders, ask, 'What can I do to fix this?' and feel the weight of the added burden. Live your life in the question. Ask yourself 'What would need to happen?' 'What would need to happen for my customers to be

surprised?' 'What would need to happen for us to win this contract?' 'What would need to happen to increase revenue by 20 percent? Other questions include 'What would it take for more of this fun to show up in my life?' and 'How can this get even better?'"

Ask "How are things going?"

You can learn so much by asking one simple question: 'How are things going?' Make a practice of walking the floor, go to your office and pick up the phone regularly to seek input from both customers and employees. Talking with both of these stakeholder groups is key to understanding if priorities and initiatives, and even concerns, are aligned. There is no substitute for real conversations to keep you grounded to what is truly happening -- and what needs to happen -- in your organization.

Don't judge an idea by its cover.

Whenever someone pitches an idea to you and about your business try to listen. Remind yourself, and others, not to prejudge the idea by the person who brought it to the table, but rather to keep an open mind and judge the idea based on its merits. Put this mentality into your daily practice and you just might find the best ideas come from the most unlikely sources.

Know the news.

At least once a week, make sure you are up to speed with industry news. See what's out there and if there is anything evolving. This is how you make sure that your business is up to date with the latest trends and technology and it is not slowly falling behind.

Structure your time.

Schedule all of your external meetings on Monday, Tuesday, and Friday, and the internal meetings on the other days. It means you have to switch gears a lot less, and makes your days more productive. Work on emails only early in the morning and late at night. This will allow you to focus during the day and not compulsively check your email, which can be really distracting.

Use competition as a motivator.

The most successful team members tend to have a competitive streak. Whether it's darts or the slam-dunk contests in the office (and then share online). Ensuring team members have a physical outlet for that competition keeps their energy up and builds a sense of team.

Implement a 10-10-10 routine.

First thing in the morning, spend 10 minutes reflecting on all of the encouraging things in your life, such as your family, health, work, and the people you work with. Next, spend 10 minutes journaling, writing about the wins from the day before, new ideas, progress on your goals, special things your kids have done (if you have any), and anything you could have done differently or have improved on. Finally, spend 10 minutes reading something positive. This 10-10-10 routine, suggested by Warren Rustand, will position you for success every day. It's a challenge to keep up with, but the impact it has will be significant.

Get to know your employees on a one-to-one basis.

At some point, your company will grow to the point at which you won't have the time anymore to interview every single employee. There will be people being recruited whom you have never even spoken with, and you should genuinely want to get to know them. So you can start a program of inviting new employees for lunch, maybe two or three months in, to discuss the challenges they're seeing and get direct feedback from these employees, compared with what they're used to and what they've seen work and not work. Some people don't realize this, but honest employee feedback can be the key to a successful company.

Try surfing

Surfing relies on a number of factors that are also important for professional growth: Mindfulness, judgment, decisiveness, boldness, patience, focus, planning, and velocity are keys to success in both surfing and business. You have to be prepared, thoughtful, and bold whenever you're catching a wave and in various business situations.

Get up early.

I like starting my day by getting up early, usually an hour before sunrise, doing some kind of exercise for 30 minutes, whether it's running, biking, or power walking, and then watching the sunrise. I find this daily routine not only helps to focus my mind for the day ahead but also energizes me.

Make time for family.

No matter how busy you are with work, show up at your son's football match and daughter's ballet show.

Arrive at the office before anyone else.

Get into the office early each day and go through the details before anyone else shows up. I have found that if I focus on the most important projects and tasks early and first, I can spend the day leading others and addressing topics, opportunities, or problems that were not there yesterday. If you come in later than others, they have the opportunity to control your day for you.

Make your meetings mobile.

For small, one-or two-person meetings, try to take them outdoors and on foot. There are a plethora of studies that show natural light and mobility are incredibly important to our mood, brain function, and general health. It goes far beyond the simple health benefits of walking.

FIVE WAYS TO STAY MOTIVATED AND ACHIEVE YOUR GOALS

Are you having one of those days when nothing seems to go right? Is every task you try to do harder than you thought it would be, and do you seem to encounter problem after problem along the way? We all have stressful times during our lives when everything seems to be going wrong, but it's crucial to stay positive as giving in will usually make the situation worse. Here are five ways to stay motivated and achieve your dreams:

1. Think less and act more

Stop putting off that difficult job because you're worried it will be too much for you, or you won't be able to do it. The more you worry about something you have to do, the less you will want to do it, so just making yourself get started is one of the best ways to stay motivated. You may have all sorts of excuses for not doing something, but once you make a start you'll feel so much more motivated to continue.

2. Plan your time and stick to the plan

Having a large task ahead of you, or a big project to complete, can be very daunting, and without a clear view of how much you have to do and when you are going to do it, it can be easy to get sidetracked and put things off until the last minute.

If you have a large project at work, set aside two hours at the same time each day to work on that particular job. Be clear about which tasks you want to complete during that two hours. If you are trying to get fit or lose weight, decide on two evenings a week when you are going to do an exercise class, or go to the gym, and stick to that.

3. Set yourself targets and treat yourself when you reach them

One of the easiest ways to stay motivated is to set yourself achievable targets. If you are setting up your own business, saying that you want to be earning $40k in five years time is a far away target. Break that five years down into periods of six months and decide how much you aim to be earning in each six month period, building up to the five years.

When you reach your targets, you will feel a great sense of achievement, and if you don't quite make it you can evaluate where you could improve to make sure you are on track for the next six months.

4. Mix things up a little

Boredom with the same routine can easily cause us to become unmotivated, so if you are feeling that you need a change then make one. If you are tired of going to the gym, start running in the park instead. If you always work in your home office, try relocating to the deck for a few hours. Even small changes in your routine can be great ways to stay motivated.

5. Make time to relax and avoid burnout

Many people go head-on into a project or business venture, and give it all their time and energy, only to collapse with exhaustion after six months and give it all up. One of the most important ways to stay motivated is to take time out to rest and enjoy yourself. Step back and appreciate what you have achieved, make time for a hobby, and spend a few hours with friends and family.

Perhaps some days you have planned to work, but you wake up feeling totally unmotivated. Don't take a whole day off as this will set a precedent, but it's OK to reduce the amount of work you do. Maybe decide just to work until lunchtime and take the afternoon off, but make sure you accomplish something tangible in the morning that you can be proud of to keep you motivated.

NETWORKING IS YOUR BUSINESS SUCCESS

How would you like to hear a statement like that? It's Easy! All you have to do is network. You can take all the great ways there are out there to meet, communicate, and make interactions into transactions but none will be as successful for you as networking. Nothing can every replace that face to face interaction that builds bonds between two people. No other form of contact is so strong to drive your life and your business to the greatest heights.

What is networking you may ask? There are many definitions, but it is simply connecting with people of like interests for the purpose of uncovering opportunities, sharing information and learning of best practices. You cannot do it alone. So it is imperative that one gets out and meets new people that they can get help with for information, contacts and business. You will find all parts of your life are filled with networking starting way back in kindergarten. You learn to talk to other people, learn from them and make connections that allowed you to make differences in your life.

The truism of networking is that when you talk to a person you have just met; you are not only talking to them but their network of hundreds of people too. You have got to be aware of that or you could make a critical mistake. Too often people look at name tags as they are coming up to meet someone. They see the name of the person's business and they start to make judgments. They think "oh they are a plumber, plumbers aren't going to be interested in my jewelry business" or they assume "oh I have already met several coaches or makeup retailers or whatever" and then they are already shutting down.

They are already deciding that that person isn't who they want to talk to to grow their business. That is such an inaccuracy it almost takes your breath away. What a way to lose the very business you are trying to grow. They could easily have a friend or a sister or co-worker or any number of people that need to know you. But you will never meet them if you have already prejudged who is going to be the right or wrong person to talk to. Another point to consider in this matter is that, what they are doing right now may not be what they are always going to do. And there very well may come a time when they too will become your ideal client.

Most people after they have heard the term networking from time to time get a pretty good understanding of what networking is. Some people though get a bit confused if they dwell on on what it is you should and should not do. You should be meeting as many people as possible. It is not about trying to see how many business cards you can give out in a certain time period. Yes, there is an exchange of cards, that is important but, more importantly there should be an exchanging of self. It is a time to start growing a relationship. It is not a time to be looking for a sale. This is hard for people at times. Especially at first when you are trying so hard to get the clients you want and, you want to just get them as fast as you can. That is not how networking works.

To be the best networker you can be means you have to know the appropriate way to network. To start off, the very best way to network is to find out how you can be of service. What is it that you can do for the person standing in front of you that can help them grow their business? This is such a wonderful way to approach networking because it allows you to give of yourself and feel even better about yourself than you did before you started to network. Some people struggle with this and the best way to put this into words is, to look into your heart and find what works for you. It may be "how can I be of service to you". For others something else may work better like, "what can I do for you that you haven't been able to do for yourself". Only you know your personality and what works best for you. The main thing is be sincere and be of service and see what happens for you.

The next best thing that you can do is to be 'other focused'. Like being of service, you want to see how you can help them. This goes even further than just being of service. When you are 'other focused' you are listening intently to what the other person is saying. You are not waiting your turn or thinking about what you will say next.
Your focus is on them and what they are sharing with you. They may help you understand what your client is looking for. They may give you clues to how you can sell to them. They may simply be giving out emotions and information that will help you grow a true relationship with this person.
Always look at them and not around to see who else you could start talking to. See only them and what they are telling you. Listen, respond, and care and you will build the best relationships and

networks without ever even having to really try.

This kind of falls in with the last paragraph above and that is, that you always want to strive to be more interested than interesting. When trying to prove how interesting you are, you will often lose the person either physically or mentally as you are talking to them. But when you focus on them, and you are more interested in what they are telling you, you will see great strides in the depth and width of your network. When you are interested in someone, you will start to understand them and be able to relate to them better. Instead of taking years to form friendships, you will find that you can become 'fast friends' with them. You will know more about them and be able to understand their needs. This will aid you in helping them, serve them, and you become the person that everyone wants to be around. How would that be for growing your network if you are the one that people like to be near?

The next key question that comes up, is where do I network? Though the answer is the same as the last two questions, I am going to give some more specifics on this one. But yes, the answer is everywhere! As you know we are always so busy.

Too busy to network some may even say. That is exactly what is going to help us network is the fact that we are so busy. So when you go to your dry cleaner, or pick up donuts, or take the kids to games or scouts; those are the people you can start networking with for your business. When you have to go get groceries, go get the car worked on, or go renew your drivers license; there is your audience, your potential client to begin to grow your business. Don't waste those opportunities. Take them in hand and make the most of them. Beyond that though, you do want to do some formal networking. So what all does that entail you may ask. That means that you are going to go to and then join organizations that are based on people networking with other people and helping each other grow their businesses. Now there are hundreds of different organizations. You are going to have to determine which ones are going to work for you. Some are going to be basically the same for any type of business and some are going to be unique depending on what type of business you do.

The one that will work for any type of business is your local Chamber of Commerce. These are people in your area and they need to know that you exist, and the only way they are going to know that is if you join the Chamber of Commerce and then actually go to the meetings and events. This will not only give you the opportunity to let people know about your business, but also you can learn about other businesses in the area and see what they are doing to grow their business. There may even be some joint venture opportunities that help you gain recognition and strength in your business. Along with that you want to join groups that are associated with your type of business or even other small business groups. This can be things like eWomen network, international association of botanical gardens, etc.

No matter what your business is there are going to be networks associated with that and you need to be a part of them. Visit them first. Make sure they are going to be helpful and have great integrity before you join them. The main thing is you have got to be a part of networks to grow your business. And the information you learn and the relationships you build are going to just be phenomenal.

Okay you know the when, who and where. The next steps help you with how to network. This starts with who you are. Now that seems easy

---

enough. My name is... My company is... It does start with those basics.

Who you are also has to incorporate your target market. Admittedly some company names allow people to immediately know what you do. "Window Cleaning by Jan". That one is easy to figure out. Often though our company names don't exactly tell people what we do and that is okay. But that is also why we must include our target market in who we are. So it would be something like this: "Hi my name is Joe Smith with Doctor Time. I work with doctors who need to find more time in their life". It is direct, easy to understand, and you immediately understand who this person works with as clients. Basically you are incorporating what you have learned before in knowing what your niche is and then understanding the market that that niche is going to touch.

The next step after saying who you are, is what your uniqueness is. Some people call this the Unique Selling Point (USP) or Unique Selling Proposition. There are lots of people out there doing the same thing you are doing. Though that might not be fun to hear it is the truth.

So you have to be able to distinguish yourself from all the others out there. Why of all the people out there selling printing services should they use you? Why of all the goal setting coaches out there should they think you will do a better job? This is not always an easy part to come up with because we were taught not to brag. Well bring out the brag book because you are going to do some bragging today! People need to know why you are special. They want to know what makes you shine brighter than the other stars. So you have to let them know.

You may be thinking but that is where I get stuck. I don't what makes me unique. This is where you have play some and think some. First off a lot of your key traits are things that have been a part of your life all along and you just accept them as who you are and yet they may be the exact traits that make you unique. I had an experience that really brought this to a head for me. Back in the corporate environment where I worked, my boss at the time was giving me my review.

He was saying that I am so organized and get my work done in such a timely manner, he wanted me to write how I am able to accomplish that. I told him I just did my job. Okay that was not what he wanted from me. But I had to think about it.

REALLY think about it. In my mind I was really just doing my job.

 I began to think about what he was asking. My parents had taught me if something needs to get done, you get it done. Procrastination was not allowed. I am an avid list maker to make sure things get in order, prioritize and then get done and off the list. Even though this came very natural to me, I realized not everyone did things this way. So I was able to understand those traits and have something to give my boss that helped him understand how I accomplished what I did. So you really have to take a close look at you. What are you so good at that you don't even think about? That may be your USP.

Another way of discovering what is unique about you is to remember what you liked doing as a child. The child in all of us wants to come out and play. In the same sort of mode think of things that you like to do that is quirky. One of my neighbors built sort of upside down bikes. Okay the wheels were still on the ground but the seat and the bar were all set up differently. That was quircky. But he could have taken that quirk in many different directions. He could have taught kids how to make them and then sell them. He could have built them himself and sold them to bike shops.

The options become very open when you are doing something that you love and that makes you stand out from the crowd. If you still feel unsure, ask friends what is unique about you or what is quirky about you. You may be very surprised what comes from that, and it may be the exact thing you needed to know to make you stand out above the crowd.

The next thing you want to look at is what your benefits are. It is crucial here that you know your benefits well and that you can articulate easily. And just as important is to always be focused on the results the benefits produce, and not the how you get there. Sometimes they have to state that they have a seven step process, or they take you through so many exams or surveys to help get your results. People don't want to, nor will they focus on the benefits if they are put in that way. You want to let them know how what you do, is going to solve their painful issues.

Tony Robbins (entrepreneur, philanthropist and life coach) talks about how people only do things for two reasons; the pleasure they will get from it, or even a stronger motivator is the pain they will avoid. Take what people hate, dread or fear and find a benefit that you create through your business. Examples would be; "No more cold calls EVER!" or "Be Fit in Less Time than It Takes to Drive to McDonalds" or "Fear not, We Will Take Care of That for You". Create something that is going to stick out and make people go 'phew, now I don't have to worry about that'. People want a product or service that is going to make their lives easier, happier and results driven.

The last part of the how to network is letting people know what you need in the next thirty days. Just put it out there and you will be surprised what happens. I was at an event and when we were doing our accelerated networking, one lady was telling us she had just moved into a much bigger office and she needs file cabinets. Now that seemed like a weird request, but four of the next fifteen people that spoke, had file cabinets they were willing to give her. Isn't that great? So we all need things in our lives and not always just clients. So let the group know as you are giving your accelerated network speech (which is usually one minute) what you need, than watch and see what happens!

So now you want to take the three of the how to network items; who you are, what is your uniqueness and what are your benefits, and put them in three formats. The first is the ten second response, the second is the elevator speech and the third is the full one minute network speech.

The ten second response is when you are being announced and they can only say your name and what you do. "Hi I am so and such and I give you the courage to take chances and make changes". Something quick, direct and tells the quick story. You then want to have your elevator speech which gives you just a few more seconds so add your best benefit to that list. And then you have your accelerated network speech which includes all three items. Practice, practice, practice until each format flows easily from you but does not sound like it is memorized.

The last thing you have to do is follow up. That sounds simple, easy to do, and just makes sense right? This is the biggest mistake people make, is that they don't follow up. All networking is based on relationships you make. So if you meet someone once and then never talk to them again, it is very unlikely you will ever hear from them and then you cannot make a sale.

What should happen immediately or at least by the next day, is that you email or call each person you got a card from during a networking meeting. This step is so simple and yet here is an example of how people do not do this vital step.

I went to a four day convention recently. I got close to fifty cards. I was out of town for a couple of days so I did not get to do 'the golden rule' of immediate follow up. How many people followed up with me... one! Only one! I then got in touch with all the others I had gotten cards from, and only one other even admitted that she had meant to follow up. People aren't doing this essential step. So when you do, you really stand out among all the other people they met. It will be you that they will remember. It will be you that they give their business too. I can't emphasis this enough but if you are serious about your business you will not miss this step.

Another part of follow up is if someone asks you for information or something do not put them off. You will want to answer them quickly so they know that they are important to you and that you are efficient with your business. People have lost business because they did not follow up with a simple question or request. Don't be one of those people. Answering their questions will put you that much closer to the sale.

And the third follow up is to find out how you did after you have finished your business with a client. First, you find out if your client is satisfied. Your client is grateful that you are concerned enough to check on them. They really appreciate it. The good thing about this is if it didn't go well, you can find out immediately and take corrective action. Better that they told you, and you get a chance to resolve it, then having them tell all their friends about a bad situation. The other good thing is, if they are satisfied, you know it immediately. You feel good because they were happy. And with their permission you can even have a testimonial for your brochures or website. Follow up after the sale also allows you to learn what is working well and what might not be working as well. It helps you grow and change your business so that it gets better and better all the time. Follow up will lead you to huge successes.

Networking can make the difference in how big and how fast your business will grow. It can allow you to quickly express yourself and your business.

It gives you the opportunity to start relationships with people that can make all of the difference in the world. Networking is a connecting life force that will make your life dynamic and your business fulfilling.

RELYING ON SOCIAL-MEDIA MARKETING IS A LOSING STRATEGY

Most of the large social media companies are now publicly traded, which means they are focused on generating profits more than ever before. For the entrepreneur, this means to reach your audience, you will have to pay to do so.

The changes in social media mirror those that happened in SEO a few years ago. There were entrepreneurs that built entire businesses on SEO, and after two Google algorithm changes, many of those businesses were wiped out. History is repeating itself with social media.

Smart entrepreneurs can weather this storm by not making social media their main marketing strategy. Here are three reasons why.

1. The organic reach will continue to decrease

As these companies continue to report their earnings, the pressure to increase profits will force them to charge for services that have been free. Organic reach may never reach zero, but it will continue to get close. There are ways to increase engagement, but if a smaller base initially sees your posts, this will become nearly impossible to do without paying to boost your posts.

For small business owners, this is not good news. The biggest problem is that paying for social media ads doesn't always translate into income, and there has been some convincing evidence questioning the effectiveness of these ads. This doesn't mean we should abandon social media, but we have to be smart about where we spend our time and money.

2. The platforms aren't yours

When you build a large social media following, you have to realize that those people are their customers, not yours. They may be following you, but that social media platform has complete control of what they see and do. Building your business on someone else's platform has led to the downfall of many entrepreneurs.

Social should be a lead generator with the ultimate goal of getting those leads to visit your website and sign up for your email list. Email marketing is still the most effective way to close the sale. After all, 100 percent of people on your email list will receive your emails without you paying to reach them.

When you can get those leads off of social media and onto your website, they have the chance to see everything you offer. This gives you the best chance to make multiple sales and create life-long customers. Your website should be your foundation not social media.

3. A diverse strategy ensures success

A diverse marketing strategy is the best marketing strategy. When SEO started to decrease, savvy entrepreneurs pivoted because they weren't too dependent on any one strategy. These same entrepreneurs will also weather the changes on social media and whatever is the next "big thing." Putting all your eggs in one basket is recipe for disaster. Social media marketing should be one part of a unique and diverse marketing strategy. If that part of the strategy starts to decrease, you pivot instead of feeling the effects financially. Successful entrepreneurs are trendsetters not followers of what used to work.

Milan Kundera (a French novelist) said, "Business has only two functions - marketing and innovation." You may have the marketing covered with social media, but if that's your only form of marketing, you're missing the innovation. A diverse strategy thrives on innovation.

These social media changes, and the ones to come, will affect your business one way or another. You have the power to decide how your business will be affected.

LISTEN TO YOUR CUSTOMER - "TELL ME SOMETHING I DON'T KNOW"

"Listen to your customer. Change your product to meet the customers' needs or change your market." You have heard this from every business advisor in the business industry.

Kathleen Dahlberg (Founder of numerous companies and currently the CEO and Founder of oVention, a technology firm ensuring hard returns on technology) says that "entrepreneurs spend too much time creating their product and not enough time selling it. They must change the product to meet the demands and needs of the customer. If the customer doesn't like it, it doesn't matter what you think of it. They won't buy it." Great, what if the customer doesn't know what she or he wants?

How do you get the right balance of what they want and what makes sense from a profit perspective? How do you know what they will want in the future? "This is tough stuff" says John Fox (President of Venture Marketing and author of "The Marketing Playbook". Venture Marketing is a marketing consulting firm focusing on its client's top line revenue)

Kent Nelson (CEO of HRH Illinois; formerly TJ Adams. HRH is the 8th largest insurance brokerage in the U.S.), recognized most of his competition (insurance brokerage) used the simple approach of shopping for expiration dates and quoting lower prices to find new business. That solved the customer's cost issue, but only until the next broker came along with a lower price.

But the customer has many more issues than just cost. In response, his commercial property and casualty business offered safety classes, introduced wellness classes, and provided blood screening to small businesses. The "value added" was obvious to the customer and shopping price quickly evaporated. Customers no longer jumped to another insurance broker because HRH offered so much more. "Cross-selling" eliminated the price war, and everyone within HRH selling each of the services participated in the commission. Nelson's customers didn't know they wanted wellness classes and blood screens. But it has broadened their attitude toward their insurance broker and the value they offer.

Nelson has now expanded his brokerage service to include an HR outsourcing solution for small business (5 to 2500 employees). By introducing these different services, HRH has multiple "points of value" with prospects. It's no longer just quoting premiums, but truly hassle free solutions in areas small businesses can't afford to hire independently.

Ben Carnevale (Former President of Oxford International, a high growth Chicago based multinational corporation serving the OEM automotive industry) says, "Keep an open mind and recognize the opportunity provided by the relationship. By working hard to understand Chrysler and working closely in a 'give and take' relationship, we saw needs well ahead of our competition." Oxford's close communication with Chrysler allowed them to develop technology that solved problems. "We began combining elements that led to higher efficiency within Chrysler. We saw the need for automation and delivered the first automated plant of the 80s." The result was a better, more competitive product for both Oxford and Chrysler. But the customer doesn't always know what they want. What then? John Fox tells the story of a major manufacturer of garage door openers who sold millions of remotes each year, but failed to see the automotive industry offering the remote as a standard item in newer cars. Now, they sell less than 100,000 remotes a year. The customer could not have told them this.....so how should they have known what the customer wanted?

Oxford's thorough understanding of the automotive industry not only brought better efficiency to Chrysler, Chrysler saw them as a problem-solver. "Here is how we did it. We sent three people into the assembly line to study their process and what happened to our product when it went in? We noticed we could reduce cost on packaging, we could provide a lighter product, and better quality was the result. We were perceived as going beyond the scope of the vendor - just by listening."

So what's the, so what, of all this? How do you listen to the customer when they don't know what they want? Your success is tied to the questions you are not asking as well as the ones you are. What does that mean? Instead of merely asking the customer what they want, become the customer for a day. Invest time in understanding them...and their businesses. Ask them how they do things? Why they do them? How much it costs to do them? What keeps them up at night? What are their priorities for the next 12 months? If they could change three things about their business what would they be?

WHY YOU SHOULD ASK FOR CUSTOMER FEEDBACK

Twenty, even ten years ago, when a complaint was usually made by letter, a dissatisfied customer could be handled in-house without anyone outside the company knowing, but those days are gone. Customers want to be valued and you can easily achieve this by reaching out to them.

Here are 5 reasons why you should ask for customer feedback.

1. Social media rules. While social media is used by companies to promote their brand, it is also used by customers to express either approval or dissatisfaction with a company's particular product or service. A bad review left on social media has the potential to go viral and do major harm to a company's image.

2. Testimonials. Customers look for social proof that a product or service is worth paying money for. Asking for feedback from customers is a great way of acquiring positive testimonials for a business. These can form part of your website

content and marketing materials to show potential customers that other customers have been satisfied with the goods or services received.

3. Increase in sales. This is the Holy Grail of every business, and positive customer feedback shared publicly, can generate more sales. No marketing is more successful than word-of-mouth recommendations, so asking for customer feedback can help to spread the word about what you are selling.

4. Improve your services. This is where a negative review, though unwelcome, can be helpful. If a customer posts a review of a product or service that examines its failings or disappointments, this information can tell you how that particular product or service can be refined or improved.

5. Improve relations with customers. Customers want to feel they are being looked after and are valued. If you ask for customer feedback, you are proving that you care what your customers think and are eager to implement changes to enhance their experience with you.

However, before you begin a customer feedback initiative, you should determine what your objective in seeking it is, by answering three basic questions:

Do you want to know how your customers feel about your company in general, or do you want specifics?

How are you going to obtain customer feedback - by letter, by phone, by email or other, such as Survey Monkey?

Once you have the feedback, how are you going to use it?

Some might argue that asking for feedback from customers is akin to asking for trouble, but there are significant benefits to finding out what buyers think of your goods or services. With ever-increasing competition between businesses, companies need to do everything they can to make their customers want to keep buying from them.

Useful Tips To Improve Customer Feedback

Feedback from its customers is very important to a company. It tells them if their customers are satisfied or not. It also gives the company the chance to get detailed views and opinions from their customers. It is necessary for a company to see where they are going wrong and what they can improve on. It is essential for you to start using email marketing to get to know your customers better. A great way to collect feedback from customers is through surveys.

The designing of a questionnaire is important. The first thing you have to think of is what you want to find out from your customers. Do you want to find out why sales have gone down or do you want to try to create a new product? When you know what you want to achieve from the survey, you can create a questionnaire based on your objectives. Don't waste time asking irrelevant questions or your customer will get bored and stop filling it out.

Designing your questions is also important. There are different types of questions to use based on what you want to find out from the customer. Examples of questions are open ended questions, Likert-scale, multiple choice and categorical questions. Open-ended questions allow you to find out more detailed information from your customer. For example an open-ended question could be, "Which one of our products is the best and why?" A Likert-scale question measures a customers attitudes towards a subject on scale from 1 to 5, one being don't like and 5 being like very much.

This type of question is good for asking opinions on a company's products. A multiple choice question allows you to find out for example which of the company's products is the most popular. Categorical questions help put your respondents into categories such as gender and age bracket. All questions should have an I don't know or not sure answer.

Questionnaires should be kept concise, the less questions the better. If a survey is too long, the customer will get bored and not finish it. It is important to use natural and familiar language so it is not too complicated for your respondents. Customers should be informed why the company is conducting the survey and what objectives they aim to achieve.

This keeps the relationship between the customer and company strong as the customer feels as though they are involved someway with decisions in the company. Analysing the findings is essential as otherwise it was a waste of time conducting the survey. If the survey was designed well, the findings should help the company meet the objectives set out at the start.

FREEBIE PROMOTIONS - HOW GIVING AWAY FREE STUFF CAN BOOST YOUR BUSINESS

It's true! Who doesn't like to get free stuff, no matter how cheap, lame or otherwise undesirable? You know it, I know it and you can be darn sure the marketing departments at the big boys out there know it and thrive on it. So why aren't YOU getting in on this?

Giving away promotional freebies is a great way to get people to buy from you, to sign up for newsletters, to get a heap of free advertising and to generally boost the profile of your business both in the online and offline world. Thankfully, in the online world, these kinds of promotions need not cost a fortune either which again begs the question: Why aren't you doing this already! Here's a few reasons why giving away free stuff is such a wonderful thing for your business.

Freebie & Coupon Sites

There are thousands of websites, forums, blogs, newsletters and other online communities who report on nothing but all the freebies currently out there on the internet. If you are giving away something free then these guys will find out about it and will more than likely list what you are giving away on their own sites. That's free advertising for your business and it'll be seen by THOUSANDS of potential new customers! It'll also do no harm to your link popularity and hence search engine rankings...

Turning The Maybe's Into The YES PLEASE's!

How many customers do you think hit your site each day, look at what you are selling, umm, ahh and then leave without buying? Why not give them a very good reason to buy from you, right there and then, rather than chancing to fate they might find your competitor's site in the meantime or decide, perhaps, they won't purchase what you are selling after all? A freebie promo can do this for you - just offer it as part of the purchasing deal.

Building Your Mailing List

Does no one subscribe to your newsletter? Give them a good reason by giving something away for free to newsletter readers. Easy. Make it something different each month and limit it to say, "the first few readers to email me the hundredth word in the newsletter" and you'll keep them reading too!

Increase Your Visitors - Virally

Tell-a-Friend scripts used to be a big deal but now they're not used all that much. However! Incentivize this form of viral marketing and it suddenly becomes increasingly effective. Give access to some kind of freebie if your customer tells a friend about your business and suddenly you've turned a somewhat mediocre form of marketing into a much more useful prospect. Make this freebie and small discount voucher for both the 'teller' and the friend and you've just got yourself two more customers for just a slight hit on your profit margin.

Need we go on? I expect not. If there is an area of your business you are looking to grow then I'm sure you can think of a way in which a promotional freebie, no matter how small, can help you achieve those goals.

But "is it worth it" I hear you say! Of course, but you've gotta be smart about it. DO NOT promise what you can't deliver and DO NOT promise what you can't afford. Fortunately, there are a number of things every online business can afford and here are a few ideas to get you started:

Ideas For Free Stuff Promotions

1) Vouchers, coupons, discounts codes. The simplest freebie you can ever give away. It costs you nothing as an online business (you email the coupon code to the customer rather than printing vouchers) and it can be used in many different ways. For example:

a) Encourage new customers to try out your services by offering new customers and ONLY new customers a $10 discount off their first order...when they spend $40 or more to cover your losses. So you might break even this time, or make a smaller profit, but you have probably got a new customer who'll be back next time for more.

b) Encourage people to sign up for your newsletter by offering a discount voucher for use against your products or services for all registrations. You get a newsletter registrant and a buyer all in one. Of course, you will make this pay-back time and again with each newsletter you send out.

c) Ensure a customer bookmarks your site and comes back for more. Simply give away a coupon to use against their NEXT order from you. Make sure this is redeemable for orders over a 'definite profit' level (e.g. $10 of orders over $50) and you've got a winner.

2) Ebooks and Other Electronic Media

Depending on the kind of business or service you are offering online, a free ebook giveaway can be an excellent freebie. This is particularly useful for getting people to join mailing lists and you can also offer different ebooks as part of upcoming newsletters too, in order to keep them reading. Make sure you can use the ebook in this way, however by checking with the author first. Many are more than happy for the exposure.

3) Cheap Stuff With Your Logo All Over It...

Now this one will cost you money but if used correctly can become the gift that keeps on giving. Make it something useful, especially something people will put near their computer or office and you'll be giving them a constant reminder of your services. Mouse Mats work great for this.

It will depend on your business on what you give away. For example, a toy store might want to give away a cheapo soft toy, maybe one which didn't sell or can be bought in bulk for peanuts. Slap your branding on it (put a ribbon with your internet address around its neck for example) and voila! Now this freebie becomes a viral advertising machine because these things get left on buses, given away to charity shops, handed down to younger children and so on.

4) Free Services and Samples

Giving away samples of your services is a great way of showcasing your talents and encouraging people to buy. This works particularly well with intangible products, like graphic design services for example. I would advise caution giving samples of physical products however, as many people will grab anything they can regardless of whether they are in the slightest bit interested in what you have to offer, and this could give you a real headache in terms of costs and the time spent packaging and mailing.

SEVEN ALTERNATIVE SOURCES OF CAPITAL FOR SETTING UP A BUSINESS

Borrowing from banks is every small entrepreneur's nightmare. One gets turned down for bank loans for a variety of reasons, including lack of assets, collateral and business experience. Don't despair, however. There are several common types of alternative sources of capital for setting up a business available to young companies.

Savings and Investments

The first source you should consider is your own savings and investments. One disadvantage though of self-financing, is that if things did not turn out the way you want them to be, it will be your money that goes down with the ship.

Angel Investors

Angel investors are affluent individuals who provide capital for a business start-up, usually in exchange for ownership equity. These individuals are looking for a higher rate of return than would be given by more traditional investments (typically 25% or more).

Angel investors are an excellent source of early stage financing and high-growth start-ups. They are often willing to tread where there is too much risk for banks and not enough profit potential for venture capitalists. And since angel investors are often retired business owners and executives, they can also provide valuable management advice and important contacts.

Peer to Peer Lending

Peer-to-peer lending is a means by which borrowers and lenders may transact business without the traditional intermediaries, such as banks. It can also be known as Social Lending, ordinary people lending money. The process may include other intermediaries who package and resell the loans--examples are Prosper.com and Zopa.com but the loans are ultimately sold to individuals or pools of individuals. Prosper.com, which is available in the US only, offers business loans for small companies.

An enabling technology for peer-to-peer lending has been the internet, which connects borrowers with lenders, for example through an auction-like process in which the lender willing to provide the lowest interest rate "wins" the borrower's loan. (wikipedia.com)

Money pool

Instead of a bank loan, borrow smaller sums from several family members, friends, or colleagues. The lenders have no legal ownership in the business, but can act as advisor and cheerleader for your venture. Remember though that nothing causes tension in a family like lending money that is never paid back.

Credit Cards

Many business owners use their credit cards to fund their businesses. Credit cards offer the ability to make purchases or obtain cash advances and pay them at a later time. But as a long-term financing method, they can be expensive. Most credit cards will charge you 2% to 4% of the face value of a cash advance as a "fee" making this method of financing very risky.

Bootstrapping

Another source of capital for setting up a business is bootstrapping. It is a way to finance a business by saving rather than borrowing money. It's being as frugal as possible so your business can be started on as little cash as possible.

The use of private credit cards is the most known form of bootstrapping, but a wide variety of methods are available for entrepreneurs. Other forms of bootstrapping include owner financing, minimization of accounts receivable, joint utilization, delaying payment, minimizing inventory and subsidy finance.

While bootstrapping involves a risk for the founders, the absence of any other stakeholder gives the founders more freedom to develop the company. Many successful companies including Dell Computers were founded this way.

Venture Capital

Venture capital is not suitable for all entrepreneurs. It is an option for small companies that have a seasoned management team and very aggressive growth plans; however, venture capitalists will rarely invest in small businesses that have no intention of going public. If a company does have the qualities venture capitalists seek such as a solid business plan, a good management team, investment and passion from the founders, a good potential to exit the investment before the end of their funding cycle, and target minimum returns in excess of 40% per year, it will find it easier to raise venture capital.

The venture capitalist objective is to invest in a company for a short period of time - say 5 years - and then cash out of the business while making a significant return on their investment.

Advantages of Business Loans

A small business loan is convenient and accessible if you have a fantastic credit rating with collateral, as well as if you agree to pay a large portion of the costs yourself. Loans help with flexibility as they only expect regular payment installments and do not monitor you on how you handle your money. It is usually more cost effective as the interest rates are usually lower than a credit card or overdrafts. You retain more profit from your business as the banks only want you to pay back the interest and loaned amount, while the rest remains in your company. A good advantage is the Tax break you get from the loan, for the interest you pay is tax deductible. However, a bank will rarely fully fund a new business and business loans are only convenient and accessible to people who do not need the money. Even with a good personal credit history, they will not give a loan for a new company, even if the company has a guaranteed contract to purchase a large order.

A business loan offers multiple loan options, but then so does a mortgage, a personal loan and a commercial card account. They are only as inventive and original as the bank wishes to make them. In many cases the true freedom is only offered to people who have long-term established business accounts with the bank, coupled with a very good credit rating.

A loan in return of a portion of the business

There are angel investors and venture capitalists who will agree to give you a loan if you give them a portion of the business. In many cases they will only accept a large portion of the company in return for a single one-time payment. They will also expect a large return from their investment and will often make restrictions or impositions on the running of the company.

The disadvantage of business loans

The biggest disadvantage of these types of loans however, is that they are almost impossible to get. Angel investors are far more likely to give to a third world startup company than a first world one, and are going to need solid proof of the businesses future success, even though that proof is impossible (in most cases) to get a hold of.

Banks do offer lower rates of interest for their loans, but they compensate for those lower charges with bigger account fees. Even depositing money into the account manually will cost the business owner money. They do offer lower rates of interests, but the account they attach the loan or overdraft to, will no doubt cost a lot of money to maintain.

Some bank loans are eligible for tax benefit, however most debt is eligible for some form of tax relief or benefit (in most countries anyway). Consider hiring a tax attorney before considering business loan tax relief a benefit.

Application process

Business loans have a very long application process. You will have to jump through a lot more hoops than you would for a personal loan. The bank will need to verify every item you put into your application and then judge your eligibility for the loan on a points system which will need to be adjusted as new information comes in. This is a very long and lengthy process.

The details that a bank needs are cumbersome and will often take you a long time to find and prove. You will need to be 100% accurate in every item of the application form and with every number you give them. This requires a lot of checking and proving which will take you a long time. Plus there are times when oversights in your accounts may damage your chance of success unfairly.

They are always going to give preference to businesses which have a long standing account with them. Unless you are one of those people, you will have to beg and plead with the bank in order to get your business loan. The many prerequisites needed for a business loan are often too difficult to obtain. Quite often the application process is nothing more than a big waste of your time and a kick in the teeth to your credit rating.

Collateral

A business loan will often ask for collateral, which they will be more than happy to take from you at the drop of a hat. A business loan is easier to revoke and demand sudden payment upon. With a mortgage they have the safety net of the house itself. They may repossess the house and make their money back. This means that they may give many warnings before taking the house.

With a personal loan, the safety net is often the fact that the loan is fairly small, and if needs be, the bank can draw out the process of getting the money back. With a business however, the tide may turn quickly. Missing a payment may be an indication that the business is on a quick decent. The bank will have to move fast and repossess your collateral as quickly as possible before it disappears.

CONCLUSION

There are many ways to succeed in business and in life, and the fastest way to get where you want is, to be open to new ideas. This book has summarised some ideas brainstormed and carefully arranged on paper especially for you. It is designed to shorten your learning curve, and spare you the time by not making the mistakes that others have done, of not listening to their employees or neglecting their families, or even worse, neglecting themselves.

It is now your decision to try out some ideas I have suggested that might better suit your personal style and your business model. I hope that you found this book useful and have enjoyed reading it as much as I have enjoyed writing it.